MORE THAN MUSIC

*How Choosing the Right Music School will
Develop Skill, Build Character,
and Prepare Your Child for a Successful Life*

Eric Nehring
and
Marty Fort

More than Music

How Choosing the Right Music School will Develop Skill, Build Character, and Prepare Your Child for a Successful Life.

ISBN: 978-1-946203-47-2

Columbia Arts Academy
3630 Rosewood Drive
Columbia, SC 29205
803-787-0931

ColumbiaArtsAcademy.com
info@ColumbiaArtsAcademy.com
Lexington School of Music
226 Barr Road
Lexington, SC 29072
803-996-0623
LexingtonSchoolofMusic.com
info@lexingtonSchoolofMusic.com

Expert Press

www.ExpertPress.net

Table of Contents

Introduction

Music Lessons Are Not Really About Music

Taking music lessons involves much more than learning to read sheet music, understanding finger placement, and refining your appreciation for sound. Music lessons provide invaluable skills that can help a student's personal, social, and academic development. A student of music can foster and develop an appreciation for being creative, confident, and persistent in their efforts to improve upon a new ambition.

Humankind has always been interested in music, even when instruments were rare and rudimentary. Music is an essential part of life that unfailingly brings us joy and elevates our spirit. In a cultural and societal sense, music is ingrained in our everyday lives. Music is a fundamental part of religious ceremonies, sporting events, and cultural festivals. It is played in coffee shops and restaurants as a soothing accompaniment to our conversations. It's an inescapable and joyous aspect of our world that is woven into our daily activities and heritage.

Since the dawn of time, music has been a vital part of the human experience. It has united people, brought about peace, and spread happiness. Music is appreciated by listeners in a variety of ways—intellectually, consciously, and spiritually. Certain songs or music styles can even work to transport a person's mind to a different time or place in their life. Music is representative of certain generations, parts of the world, and historical events. Music is a fundamental component of the human experience that expresses our intelligence, imagination, and desires.

Music lessons provide a platform for children, teens, and adults to set goals and watch them unfurl in front of their eyes. The skills learned in a music lesson or during a recital are applicable outside of the realm of just music. For example, if a student takes voice lessons, they're working to improve their tone of voice; this will, in turn, make them more confident and direct speakers in the classroom or at work. Music schools are positive and uplifting environments for students that nurture personal development. A young guitar student who sits in a mentoring session for 30 minutes will not only progress in her musical abilities, but she will also develop other essential skills, such as her attention span and practice habits. Music lessons teach students the value of completing a task once it is started. The process of following through on an entire process is a valuable skill that helps mold a student into a successful and motivated person later in life.

I have written this book for parents and prospective adult students to demonstrate what my 25 years of teaching music have shown me as an educator. If you are picking up this book, you may already be curious about putting your child in music lessons. This book will delve into my insights on music lessons as a decade-long school and academy owner. I hope that in sharing the remarkable transformations I have seen in students over the years, you will feel inspired to allow your child to pursue their own musical journey. This book is designed to help you become more educated on the process of enrolling your child in music lessons and the evolution you can expect to see in your child. I hope that you will develop an awareness of how music lessons can improve your child's life and a desire to become involved in seeing your child cultivate a new hobby.

Whether you're looking to learn more about the process for a child, friend, or a family member, my primary goal is to demystify the world of music. The information and anecdotes in this book are included to eliminate your fears, answer your questions, and alleviate any hesitation you may have in jumping into the process of beginning music lessons. This book will reveal the real-life benefits that music can have in you and your child's lives. I will explain how music schools are excellent institutions for developing personal growth and challenging oneself.

MORE THAN MUSIC

From Isolation to Influence

How a music professor helped turn an unsuspecting guitarist into a published writer

An Evening of Panic

I was staring at a blank computer screen in the basement of the Wilson Library on the West Bank campus of the University of Minnesota. I was tired. Really, *really* tired. As a second-year grad student majoring in guitar performance, I was used to making deadlines, cramming for ear training tests, and dragging myself through the Minnesota winter to make an 8:00 a.m. Post-Tonal Music Theory class. But that morning was different.

I had spent the entire night before at Minneapolis Children's Hospital. Our two-year-old son, Caleb, had recently developed croup—a severe respiratory illness—and this episode was especially traumatic. During the night, I heard him choking and gasping in his crib. We usually kept the bedroom doors open in case such an episode occurred. However, my previous experience with his illness had not prepared me for what happened next.

I entered Caleb's room to find his entire head and pillow covered in blood. His hair was soaked and matted, his eyeballs covered. I yelled to my wife, Erin, to bring me some towels. We began toweling him off and noticed that an excessive amount of blood was coming from his nose—and it was not stopping. We plugged his nose and continued to remove the blood from his face and neck. He was barely breathing. His lips were blue and his body completely limp. I panicked. Acting only on instinct, I grabbed Caleb in my arms; we loaded him into the car and sped as fast as we could to Minneapolis Children's Hospital.

This was not our first such trip in the middle of the night, but it was our most traumatic to date. Our only son was battling for every breath, and my heart sank further with his every sputter. Thankfully, the staff at Children's was able to get him the care he needed during our red-eye visit, and we returned home around 5:00 a.m. After getting Caleb back to sleep, and doing what I could to calm Erin's nerves, I had to head back down to The Cities to make a music history class.

A Charge of Plagiarism

So, once again, there I was staring at a blank computer screen in the basement of Wilson Library. I was supposed to have done some reading the night before on the origins of American roots music. Unable to recall the details, I began brainstorming some ideas I remembered about the life of the famous ragtime pianist, Scott Joplin. Still foggy in my recollection, I decided to write my professor, Karen Painter, to ask if I was interpreting the information correctly.

Dr. Painter is a highly-credentialed music history scholar. As an Ivy League graduate and former professor at Harvard University, her work is well regarded within academic circles. Needless to say, sending her a roughly composed email to clarify my understanding left me feeling insecure. I expected her to reply with a polite retort about how I had forgotten *this* important event, or how I messed up *that* particular detail. Instead, the email she sent back immediately changed my academic career.

Dr. Painter's reply did not address the specifics of my writing. Instead, she forwarded me a copy of the University of Minnesota's policy on plagiarism. Specifically, she warned that another infraction could result in expulsion!

I was stunned. "There must have been some misunderstanding," I thought to myself. Not only had I *not* plagiarized anything, my email was simply a faint recollection about the history of American roots music. I responded to Dr. Painter, apologizing for the misunderstanding. She replied with a request for a private meeting—and she wanted to speak with me prior to class *that* day. Obediently, I ensured her I would report to her office before class, and I did.

I remember entering her office. Books of Gustav Mahler and other prominent European composers lined the office shelves. The evidence of Dr. Painter's academic prowess adorned the room. As I sat down, I was prepared for the worst. Instead, Dr. Painter was very calm and endearing.

"I apologize for my assumption," she said. "When I read your email, it read like a published author. I have never seen writing like that from a performance major. You have a gift, and you should pursue it," she asserted.

Unsure of how to respond, I told her the story of how I had been up all night in the hospital with my son. I told her his condition and how, as a father, my heart was broken for him. I told her that the email I sent was just a rough brainstorm—recalling, as best I could, some of the details of recent reading assignments.

"You should really pursue a career as a writer," she again asserted.

"I will think about it," I muttered before thanking her for her time and excusing myself from her office.

In the days that followed, I remember picking up my instrument. I was supposed to be preparing J.S. Bach's *Lute Suite in E Minor* for my upcoming master's recital. Instead, Dr. Painter's words echoed through my mind. "You should really pursue a career as a writer," continually bounced around in my head.

Later that day, I picked up a copy of the Minnesota Daily—the campus newspaper of the University of Minnesota. There was an ad stating that the paper was looking for writers. I had never written anything before outside of class assignments, but Dr. Painter's words continued to resonate. So, I decided to take the plunge and submit an application. For my writing portfolio, I submitted some rough notes I had compiled during Dr. Painter's Music History class, including the email I had recently sent her. The submissions were not *exactly* application material, but it was all I had. In the following days, much to my surprise, I received a response back indicating I had been selected for an interview.

The View from the Third Floor

Days later, I made the trek across campus to an unfamiliar building adjacent to TCF Bank Stadium. The sign next to the entrance indicated the Minnesota Daily was located on the third floor. I remember clenching my jaw as I ascended the elevator. My hands were sweating and my heart was racing. When I entered the conference room and met with the senior editor, Jake, everything became enhanced.

Jake was a well-groomed young man in his early twenties who appeared very comfortable in his position. I was a 32-year-old grad student who was very uncomfortable in mine. When he asked why I wanted this position, I told him the story about the email I had sent to Dr. Painter. He responded, "You know, most of our applicants are J-School majors who are preparing for a career in journalism. You submitted some rough notes about Scott Joplin and the origins of Ragtime music?" The pitch of his voice raised slightly at the end of the phrase suggesting he questioned the credibility of my application.

"I know," I said apologetically. "Maybe I jumped the gun? I probably shouldn't have applied," I continued. ("There are surely people better suited for this position than me," I thought to myself.)

Almost certain the interview was over, I arose from my chair, and extended a handshake to thank Jake for his time.

"Take a seat," he said. "I have a few more questions for you."

Unsure of what would follow, I sat back down and did as he suggested.

I honestly can't remember the remainder of his questions, or my responses to them. But at the end of the interview, Jake offered me a job as an Op/Ed columnist for the largest college newspaper in the United States. I was floored. Moments later, Jake shook my hand and left the corner conference room. I remember smiling from ear to ear as I stood there alone, gazing out the window across the beautiful U of M campus nestled in the foreground of downtown Minneapolis. In that moment, I knew I had been granted an opportunity that would shape the rest of my life.

The Transformation

After accepting the position, I had much work to do. I had never really read a newspaper before, so I began devouring every paper I could find. I turned on the news, clipped out magazine headlines, and began studying reputable journalists. By the time I was supposed to submit my first article pitch, my head was spinning.

The next day, I met Jake in the news room to pitch him my ideas. We kicked around some thoughts and eventually emerged with a topic. Suddenly, the clock was ticking. I had less than 24 hours to submit a fully-edited, polished piece that was going to debut in front of more than 20,000 readers. The pressure was intense. That day, I locked away my guitar, skipped Music History class, and grabbed the corner table in the West Bank Campus Starbucks. I typed, deleted, sipped coffee, typed, deleted, *slammed* coffee—the process continued for hours.

By the time I arose, my legs were nearly asleep yet jittering from the caffeine. Now, it was time to make the submission. As I made my way across campus to submit my column, the bitter February wind gave me a chilling moment of pause.

"Am I doing the right thing?" I asked myself as I crossed the bridge high above frozen Mississippi River.

"I should be focusing on my guitar studies, yet I just spent the afternoon researching Michelle Bachmann's "Light Bulb Bill," I thought to myself.

Part of me wanted to scrap the idea, call Jake and tell him I wasn't cut out for this, and return to the practice room where I felt comfortable. Yet, I kept walking. Thankfully, that afternoon I somehow found the courage to submit my work. In less than 48 hours, the column was going to appear before 20,000 readers.

The Debut

The morning it went to print was much like any other morning. I woke up at 5:00 a.m., took a shower, and fixed myself a bowl of Cheerios and two pieces of buttered wheat toast. I then drove to my grandmother's house to practice guitar for 90 minutes before heading to the 95th Ave Park and Ride to catch the 252 to campus.

The ride to campus was the usual. Traffic…snowplows…darkness. But as the bus came to a stop along University Ave, the knot in my stomach grew bigger. Moments later, I jumped off the bus and approached the paper kiosk adjacent to the building entrance. Almost afraid to look, I grabbed a copy and went inside.

I made my way to my usual spot in the basement of the Wilson Library. Before I opened the paper, I reflected on the moment—just a couple weeks prior—in which I sent the email to Dr. Painter. Had it not been for the sleepless night in the hospital, the roughly composed email about Scott Joplin, or the subsequent assumptions regarding plagiarism, I would never have become a published columnist. But those events had passed, and it was time to read my work—in print.

As my eyes consumed the final line of text, I experienced a mix of emotions. Fear, joy, intimidation, uncertainty.

"How are people going to react?" I thought. After all, the piece was opinion journalism covering a controversial legislative bill authored by, arguably, the United States' most controversial congresswoman. That question was answered the moment I checked in at the music office that morning.

"I read your column," the receptionist quietly remarked.

"Thank you," I replied. "What did you think?"

She responded with an almost guilty smile, suggesting she enjoyed the column but didn't want to reveal to her colleagues that she had been reading Op/Ed pieces on the job.

From Isolation to Influence

In that moment, something in me changed. Regardless of how people reacted to my column, I felt a sense of accomplishment. I had made a difference. I gained a sense of influence. I went from the isolation of a college music department practice room, to the pages of the most-read college newspaper in the country—without training, without preparation, and without a plan. But what I *did* have was a voice in the back of my head from Dr. Painter saying, "You should really pursue a career as a writer." Though I had a long way to go before eventually establishing myself as a columnist, I had taken the all-important first step.

In the months that followed, I continued my pursuit of writing and of journalism. I was fortunate to get to interview two former Minnesota governors and attend conferences alongside reporters from C-SPAN, CNN, FOX News, Reuters, and the New York Times—just to name a few. Further, my subsequent columns became, according to Jake, some of the most engaging in the history of the paper. Not bad for a guitarist from the tunnels of the West Bank!

Though my career as an Op/Ed writer eventually gave way to the demands of my performance career, the skills I gained during that period of my life remain with me today. As the founder, owner, and director of Minnesota School of Music, I now publish one of the largest hard-copy music education newsletters in Minnesota—the Monthly Musician. Each month I have the opportunity to collaborate with a team of talented professionals to share my stories, and to deliver actionable information to Minnesota School of Music customers. To receive your copy of The Monthly Musician, simply visit our website at

www.mnschoolofmusic.com and submit the Request Info form. We'll mail you out a copy right away!

The Real Value of Music Education

I share this story with you not to build myself up, or to brag about how I went from being a nobody to a somebody on one of the largest college campuses in the United States. I share this story because it is a story of a young grad student who was encouraged by a university professor to pursue his passions, even though they resided outside the field of music. It is a story of uncertainty, of fear, of isolation, and ultimately of hope and triumph. I went in a guitarist and came out a writer!

In the same way, if you are looking to enroll your child in a music school, you and your child may feel fearful and uncertain. Music lessons may feel awkward at first. After all, they are something new. Quite honestly, you may ultimately discover your child does not share a passion for music. However, when a student is in the presence of a highly-skilled professional teacher (like Dr. Painter), it's possibile for untapped talents to be discovered.

Perhaps your child will one day grace the stage of Carnegie Hall. Perhaps not. Perhaps they will create their own YouTube channel and become an internet sensation. More than likely, they won't. But what I can guarantee is that if they enroll in a high-quality music school, they will learn important life skills. They will learn to overcome challenges, to believe in themselves, and to pursue their passions, wherever they reside. In short, the study of music can lead to some truly lifechanging opportunities. It sure did for me!

In the pages that await, one of my friends and mentors shares his valuable expertise in what to look for in music school. I have known Mr. Marty Fort for almost 6 years, and I can think of no other individual that I would rather call a co-author than him. His knowledge of the music education industry has placed him in a class by himself. Much of what I know about how to run a music school has come directly from his mentorship.

So, whether you are the mother of a 7-year-old looking to enroll in first-time piano lessons or a 17-year-old high school junior preparing for a college audition, the wisdom and insight shared by Mr. Fort in the following pages is invaluable. As you begin your search for a highly skilled music teacher, consider this book your map. By following Mr. Fort's guidance, your child will end up in the care of a professional music teacher that will help them achieve their dreams. I truly hope your child's musical journey will be as rewarding as mine!

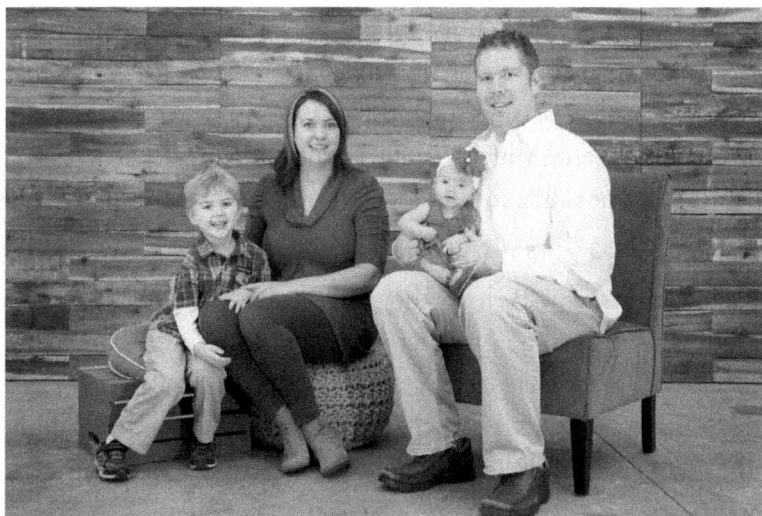

MINNESOTA
SCHOOL OF MUSIC

3533 88th Ave NE
Blaine, MN 55014
(763) 432-9713

Chapter 1.

You Are Their Greatest Teacher
(What You Can Do at Home)

Nobody spends more time with a child than their parents or caretakers. For this reason, a child's first teachers are their parents, because they instill morals and provide guidance in the child's early life. Just like teaching a child to read or write, playing music in the home can have a positive impact on the development of your young one. I think it is essential to frequently play music in the home because it can spark a child's curiosity and, naturally, is a great source of entertainment.

There are a variety of simple ways that you can incorporate music into your daily routine. Just as many parents have dedicated story time with their young ones, playing music can (and should) become a regular part of your day. By turning on the radio, a music channel on TV, playing music on your computer, or even singing songs yourself, you can engage with your child in new and exciting ways. I encourage parents to structure an everyday routine of playing music in the house or having their child sing along with their favorite songs.

The daily reinforcement of any activity helps children feel more comfortable and secure, because their daily activities are predictable and familiar. You can have music playing when changing diapers, before nap time, or during bath time. An appreciation for music can begin in the earliest stages of life.

By singing nursery rhymes to your child, no matter what you think of your own singing voice, the bond with your child will deepen, and the exposure to new sounds will benefit their health and well-being. Background music can also be played at certain times of day, like when a child is working on arts and crafts, during mealtime, or in the car. No private teacher can spend as much time with your child as you do. You can reinforce the values that a music teacher teaches during lessons by establishing a routine of playing music throughout the entire day.

Sound and vocal interaction with your child is important for a baby's developing brain. When a baby cries, they can expect to get attention from their parents as a result of the noise they create. This sequence of output and recognition formulates a pattern in a baby's mind. They can expect to receive the same repeated attention after conveying a certain behavior.

Babies easily adopt habits as they learn to predict what the outcome of a certain situation may be. In this way, singing can be used as a positive tool to promote a sense of calm and safety in your child. If you sing to your child while they are crying, they'll feel comforted by your conscious attention to their needs. Eventually, they will sing back to you and respond to this communication in a positive and mutually-beneficial way.

By playing music in the home, you're building a foundation for your child's future. Engaging in this habitual mechanism conditions your children to express themselves, their preferences, and their wishes from an early age.

Along these lines, I also recommend that parents keep instruments in the home for older children, ages five and above. A child's natural curiosity may lead them to picking up an instrument and explore it. By having instruments in the house that promote a positive expression of their curiosity, you're allowing for your child's interests to expand. They may be motivated to learn the instrument, and you may wish to sign them up for music lessons at some point. Your influence can help introduce your child to music organically and naturally.

Chapter 2.

You Have a Tin Ear, Can't Sing, Can't Dance, and Other Myths

In the past, you may have been told by someone you have a tin (or musically insensitive) ear. Perhaps you feel that you can't sing or dance to a beat. You might have allowed your insecurity to convince you that you are tone-deaf or musically unskilled. These are all falsehoods that you might have accepted as the truth.

Fortunately for you, I'm here to inform you that being a good at an instrument is not a gift bestowed upon you at birth. Everyone has the ability to improve their musical skills and become a more talented singer, dancer, or musician.

Being persistent and taking the time to practice are attributes of all great musicians and artists. Just because you feel you aren't talented at an instrument does not mean that you cannot learn to play one.

For adults who are just starting to learn to play an instrument, patience with yourself is key. A 60-year-old family friend of mine approached me and expressed his desire to begin taking voice lessons. I told him his biggest obstacle in pursuing voice lessons would simply be showing up. Adults are constantly pulled in different directions by their busy lives. Hobbies like voice lessons are usually the first commitment that adults cancel when they are busy.

The second biggest obstacle would be forgiving himself for natural failures. If events in his life become overwhelming and he were to miss several weeks, it's important for him to be patient with himself and know that he doesn't need to quit just because his attendance has been inconsistent. If he quits, he won't be able to realize his dreams; but if he persists and is mentally committed to attending a certain amount of lessons per year, he will be that much closer to achieving his goals.

Whether it is children or adults seeking to attend my music academy, I inform all potential students that success in their music lessons isn't just about the music, but rather about their perspective toward the journey.

As a musician, songwriter, teacher, and professor in the field of music, I have witnessed thousands of students transform their lives and grow in ways they never thought were possible.

Many students experience slow and gradual improvement, but their persistence and dedication allow for breakthroughs in their skills that many less motivated students never experience.

For this reason, I ask that parents let their child's journey move forward organically, not to hold their child to an expected schedule of "achievement". Learning to play music is a living, breathing process that begins with you as the parent simply asking the child to play a song for you.

Chapter 3.

Signs Your Child is Ready for Lessons

A child often conveys readiness for music lessons with *physical expression*. This is often starts with banging on pots and pans, tapping on couches, pretending a briefcase is a piano or that a notebook is a keyboard. If you play music and your child stops what they're doing and starts dancing, that's a good sign that they might have an interest in music.

The next sign that your child is ready for lessons is usually through *verbal expression*. The child may tell you outright that they want to start playing an instrument or taking voice lessons. Once the physical and verbal interest is there, it's up to you as a parent to get the ball rolling. Our school is unique in that it offers month-to-month payment options for families. We don't require long-term contracts or commitments like other music academies or sports programs.

When searching for a school, choose one with a month-to-month or short-term payment plan. If your child enjoys their lessons, they can continue. If they're not, you can submit a withdrawal form. Don't go to a school that requires you to sign long contracts. You should also be wary of schools that require a substantial pre-payment before you begin lessons.

The schools with the best teachers are flexible and have month-to–month plans that do not require stiff contracts. Good schools also have the option for electronic payments. Find a school with a month-to-month auto-pay service, and if the lessons do not work out, you can put in your notice and find something else your child is more interested in.

Chapter 4.

What is the Right Age to Begin?

Every music teacher has their own opinion about the appropriate age to start children in music lessons. For this reason, the topic can be quite controversial. Children have many different levels of development. Their attention span, listening skills, and dexterity are all constantly developing and changing, which often makes it difficult to focus on learning music.

My music school has over 1,200 students, and our students' parents are comfortable with our age guidelines for each instrument we offer. For piano, we allow children to begin taking lessons at age four. For the guitar, we permit children to start at age five. Kids can start learning the drums at age six (if the child can reach the pedals). Voice lessons also begin at age six.

Our month-to-month payment agreement allows for flexibility and breaks should the student's schedule or interests change. If a child starts with a particular instrument and it doesn't work out, the family can withdraw the student, take a break, and return when the child and parents feel they're ready.

I've seen many kids try an instrument, tell their teacher they want to try a different one and thrive. Part of the organic learning process with music is that a person's efforts and interests are not expected to be consistent and unchanging.

We understand that a child's curiosity fluctuates over time, and we make it our mission to help them explore the instruments that interest them the most.

Chapter 5.

How to Choose a Teacher

When it comes time to select a music teacher, you will need to consider whether you'd rather have your child take in-home lessons or lessons at a music academy.

There are numerous benefits in enrolling your student an academy. One of the primary advantages is that your child will be surrounded by other excited students, which works as a valuable source of inspiration for young learners.

Additionally, your child will benefit from hearing other instruments and having the opportunity to touch, hold, and feel other instruments. Inspiration and sensory stimulation in the form of touch, sight, and sound are positive factors that promote a child's development. Students who take lessons at home won't be able to see other children at various skill levels practicing. If they don't have exposure to other students, they cannot be inspired to improve their abilities by watching others excel at playing their chosen instruments.

We encourage students who are homeschooled to attend a music academy so that they can have the opportunity to be influenced positively by their peers. Children who are homeschooled often have a more flexible schedule and they can take their lessons during the midday lunch hours while other students are at school.

It is important to select an academy that places emphasis on recitals. At our academy, we have recitals every six months where students are able to perform in front of other students and their families. We have numerous achievement programs, including the Musical Ladder System® (which will be discussed in greater detail in this guide). The music achievement program allows students to earn wristbands and trophies for their successes during recitals. This type of positive recognition of hard work boosts a student's self-esteem and encourages other students to work harder and accomplish even more.

The experience of learning to play an instrument is often collaborative. When you are starting a new workout regimen, it's much easier to be motivated at a gym where you're surrounded by other people working hard rather than working out at home. In music schools, the experience of being in an environment with other musicians can enrich a student's experience and deepen their appreciation for their own instrument.

As mentioned in the earlier chapters, do your vetting before selecting a music school. Be sure to ask the school some of the following questions to get a better idea of how they manage and what they value:

● How many years have you been in business?

● Are you the largest school in the area?

● Do you offer a variety of instrument options for students?

- Do you have office staff present at all times for every lesson?

- Do you have a family safety plan in place?

- Do you offer recitals and are there recital fees?

- Do you have incentivizing achievement programs?

Once you have asked these questions and have gotten the answers you need, you will be able to select the right school for your child.

We ask that students fill out a questionnaire before their first lesson so that the teacher can get a general idea of what the student wants to accomplish.

When choosing an academy, be sure to choose one that has multiple teachers for multiple instruments. This way if you start with a particular teacher, and it isn't a perfect fit, you can transition to another teacher without leaving the academy.

Chemistry between a child and a teacher will develop over time as the child grows. A student may have an excellent relationship with their current teacher and then one day have a substitute and realize they like that person even better.

The sign of a good teacher is one who keeps the parents in the loop and continually communicates a student's struggles, progresses, and development.

Before selecting a teacher, be sure to ask the important questions, take a tour of the facility, and choose the person who best reflects your own philosophy on learning.

MORE THAN MUSIC

Chapter 6.

Should My Teacher Have a Degree?

Some of the greatest music teachers I have encountered during my life in the music industry have not had a music degree. I have also encountered many well-educated teachers with PhDs that, in my opinion, didn't really care about the students and were poor communicators. **I do not put emphasis on a teacher's resume or degrees.**

In some areas of music, such as in piano and violin, you tend to encounter teachers that are more credentialed than others. Many will have advanced degrees due to the complex nature of their instruments. In contrast, the majority of drum teachers, for example, did not even attend college for drums.

At my school, we ask that all new students complete a questionnaire as part of their registration. We try to learn why new students are interested in music lessons, who they are, and what their goals are.

The first lesson is largely exploratory and conversational as the teacher and family become acquainted with one another. The teacher is attempting to determine what the student is like and what their interests are.

After the questionnaire and initial lesson, the student may declare that they want to learn to play a specific song, perform at a wedding, or maybe dye their hair green and join a punk rock band.

If this is the case, then that particular student might not need to know how to read music. Instead, the punk rock student would work on strengthening their fingers and learning chords to songs by The Ramones. I think it's a disservice to the individual student if a teacher standardizes the curriculum. The teacher should listen to a student's interests and needs and develop a curriculum that will help them achieve their specific goals.

On the other hand, the questionnaire may reveal that the student wants to go to a major university and be a music major. In this case, the student would definitely benefit from an ability to read music fluently, understand music theory, and play classical and popular music.

A good music teacher will be able to quickly understand what a student is interested in. If your child has a substitute teacher, you won't need to explain your whole life story to them. They will ask what kind of music the student likes and will identify within a few minutes what level the child is at.

Good musicians and good teachers will be able to assess the information you give them and create a curriculum that fits your goals.

Chapter 7.

Should My Child Learn How to Read Music?

I believe all music students should learn how to read music, but this again depends on the instrument and the age of the student. If a student is a young child and they want to learn piano, violin, or guitar, they should absolutely learn how to read music. This may not be as important if they're an older student, and if they are interested in playing an instrument like guitar or bass.

I am a guitar player, I read music, and I taught as a professor to college-level students who were required to read music and theory. But if a student is 13 or 14 and wants to learn Van Halen, I don't believe they need to learn to read music at all. There are very few rock bands playing concerts with a lead guitarist on stage and reading sheet music while playing a solo. The same theory goes for teenagers who are reaching high-school age. If they want to be heavy-metal guitar heroes, reading music is not as important as simply learning to play.

My attitude towards learning to read music is that young children should be exposed to as much music as possible and should definitely learn to read music. As they get older, especially with adult students, learning to read notes does not matter as much.

Chapter 8.

Should My Child Major in Music?

Parents often ask me if their child should become a music major in college. In 2008, I finished my Masters in Guitar Performance from USC; in 1997, I completed my Bachelor of Music in Guitar Performance from the University of North Carolina School of the Arts. I've definitely put in my time in for the academic side of music and have formulated some strong opinions regarding what is beneficial and what is not from this experience.

When a parent asks me this question, it usually means that their child is 17 or 18, college is looming, and they need to decide on a major. The student may not really know what they want out of college, but they do know that they love to play music. In their minds, being a music major would be fun; they could play a lot more music, and it would be an easy way to get through college (as opposed to studying math or science, for example).

Unfortunately, this is an unrealistic outlook. Music studies at the college level are intense. They are also largely antiquated, with a focus on classical music or, at best, a jazz program. Johnny may love to rock out on his Les Paul and learn Metallica riffs at the Academy, but no college in South Carolina allows you to take rock guitar lessons in a music school. I was one of the first (if not only) professors to teach rock guitar at the University of South Carolina Upstate, where I taught a variety of guitar and music courses.

If you are going to major in music, you must be able to pass a classical or jazz audition, and now is the time to start practicing!

There are two reasons that I feel a student should major in music in college. The first is if they want a career as a teacher. If you are going to teach in a college, you must have a degree in music performance or music education. If you want to teach in a high school, middle school, or elementary school, you must have a degree in music education, pass the state Praxis exam, and become certified to teach music.

If this is the route you want to take, you must be proficient in either classical or jazz because there is no "rock or pop" program at USC or any other college in South Carolina. As an alternative, some parents mention the Berklee College of Music in Boston, but I feel that the school with 2,000 guitar students (versus 20 at a school like USC) and the very expensive tuition is not necessarily the best way to go for most students.

The second reason to get a degree in music is if you want to be a librarian. My wife is a media specialist librarian, and there is a job market for students with music undergraduate degrees who go on to get a Masters in Library Science.

When given these two options, many students say that they don't want to do either. They just want to play music. My suggestion for these students is to major in something practical, such as math, English, history, or another focus and merely minor in music.

As a music minor, they will still get to take music classes, it will be easier to gain admittance to the school of music, and if they still have a burning desire to become a music major, they can do so later in their studies.

The student will still need to get with their academy teacher and practice for the rigorous classical or jazz audition. The audition requirements are available on the websites of the colleges that they want to try out for. They will also need to be a good sight-reader and know some basic music theory. If your child can take a course on theory in high school, it will help.

The basic curriculum for college music majors is two years of music theory and ear training. First year music theory classes involve learning all major and minor keys, major and minor scales (and their counterparts), ancient 4-part writing, harmonic analysis, and intervals.

Second-year students analyze symphonic scores by Mozart, Berlioz, and Bach. Ear training can be a tough course for some as students learn to sing and recognize pitches, intervals, chords, and a variety of melodic and harmonic content by ear alone. Many of the exams require singing arpeggios and scales in front of a full classroom.

Performance majors will have four years of private lessons, two years of music history, and some ensemble training.

For the first year, students can get by with remedial sight-reading skills, but by the second year, they will have to show significant improvement.

Jazz majors will have classes in jazz ensemble, arrangement, jazz theory, and improvisation.

Some parents are insistent that their child pursue music scholarships and go to college for music. The challenge is that if the student has only been taking guitar lessons for five years, playing Jimi Hendrix with their teacher, and can't read a note of music, the college is not going to accept them.

If you want your child to study music in school, go to art camps, or attend governor school, they have to be able to read music and understand theory. To prepare for these high-level aspirations, you must communicate with your child's teacher, define goals, and prepare early.

Chapter 9.

Should We Rent or Buy an Instrument?

Your child's teacher will be the best source of information on whether you should rent or buy an instrument and when the time is appropriate to do so.

Do not invest in an instrument before your first lesson. Your child's teacher will help your child try out different models and sizes of the instrument and make a recommendation after the session on what you should buy.

It's also important to remember that a child's interests may change. If a child is the right age and expresses an interest in a specific instrument, such as drums, it is vital that you strike while the iron is hot and begin music lessons. You don't know whether the drums are a just phase for your child or if playing them will be a lifelong hobby.

Allowing a child to play an instrument of their choosing will reinforce the fact that they are capable of trying something new and challenging. If their interest in drums eventually wanes, they will have at least gained the confidence and satisfaction of trying something new.

The benefit of music lessons is that they are relatively inexpensive compared to other activities, such as golf, where money is required for clubs, fees, and gear. If a child starts drum lessons, most music schools will charge month-to-month.

If a child no longer wishes to play a particular instrument, we can recommend a different one. Once a child has started learning one instrument, it is not unusual for them to become interested in learning other instruments as well.

Keeping an instrument in a communal area of the home has numerous benefits. The child's interest may be piqued by seeing the instrument on a daily basis. Other family members (both children and adults) may also become interested in learning to play it. When guests visit your home, they may also express an interest in the instrument on display.

I often tell parents that they shouldn't expect their kid to sit down and play the piano in front of them for a lengthy amount of time. Instead, if you want to encourage your kid to practice, start by asking them to play a song, and if the child wishes to continue to play afterward and share their new skills, then let that be their decision. Extroverted children who love to play for others should be given the opportunity to do so, but introverts who are quiet and shy shouldn't be expected to show off to family and friends on-demand.

One of my personal mantras is: "Just because they aren't practicing today doesn't mean they won't practice one day." I maintain this viewpoint because some people take longer to come around to music than others. When parents fear that their child is not practicing enough, I remind them that each person is different. If a child attends one lesson a week for a year, the 48 lessons they've taken are certainly better than zero. I urge parents to let their children develop at their own pace and to not cut their child's potential short because they are impatient.

If your child tells you that they no longer wish to play their instrument, you have two options on how to proceed. The first option is to stop the lessons altogether, though I rarely recommend this path. The second option requires asking their school administrators for guidance.

The school will recommend that the student try a different instrument or a different teacher. Your child's teacher may also have an opinion on the next steps to take. They may recommend that they work from a different book or take a different approach to their lessons.

Students often just need to choose a different instrument to reignite their passion for music. However, if you've already explored a change in teacher or instrument, then it is my belief that a break can be healthy. If a student needs a few weeks (or a few years) away from music lessons, then they should make that decision and you should respect it. The process of learning music is not a static and flat journey. There are ups-and-downs, pauses, and surges of forward movement. Acknowledging this will make it easier for you and your child to communicate during the journey of learning to play an instrument.

When I was nine years old, I told my mother I no longer wanted to play violin. I was in the youth symphony and had lost interest in the instrument after years of playing. My mother heeded my wishes. Years later, I saw Michael J. Fox play electric guitar in *Back to the Future* and my passion for music was reinvigorated. I wanted to learn electric guitar.

My first guitar had three strings, and I would sit near the radio and attempt to mimic the melodies. I started out by playing melodies rather than playing chords, and that helped me learn to play music by ear. Later in my childhood, I was given a proper six-string guitar and began lessons. My teacher gave me a music book after my first lesson, and I never looked back. I've included this personal anecdote to show you that if interest in a specific instrument dies, that passion can still reignite at a later time with a different instrument.

Just because a student has lost interest in a particular instrument does not mean you shouldn't maintain the daily routine of playing music in the home (as I recommended early on in this book). Expose your child to a variety of different styles of music and take them to concerts. Show your child your record collection, and tell them about your favorite artists, be it the Rolling Stones or Frank Sinatra. Chances are that your kids will take a liking to the music you enjoy, especially if you play it consistently around the house.

Chapter 10.

Keeping Your Child Safe in Music Lessons (The Importance of a Family Safety Plan)

I created and designed my own music school because I felt that some extra-curricular institutions were not very safe for children. I sought to develop a wonderful, compassionate environment that had a family safety plan built into the program because safety is one of my top priorities as a father.

If you're looking to enroll your child in a music school or studio, you should ask the staff and management if they have a family safety plan in place and to provide you with an example of their plan. The features of the safety plan at my school are broken down below:

1. **Glass Windows:** We have huge glass windows on every door in our buildings to foster transparency between the teachers and parents. While it is expected that older kids and teenagers will not want their parents to sit in on every music lesson, some parents may not feel

comfortable with having their child in a separate room for a half-hour. To appease both students who wish for their lessons to be private and parents concerned about safety, we have 18" x 36" windows on every single door so that parents can view their student's lesson with peace of mind.

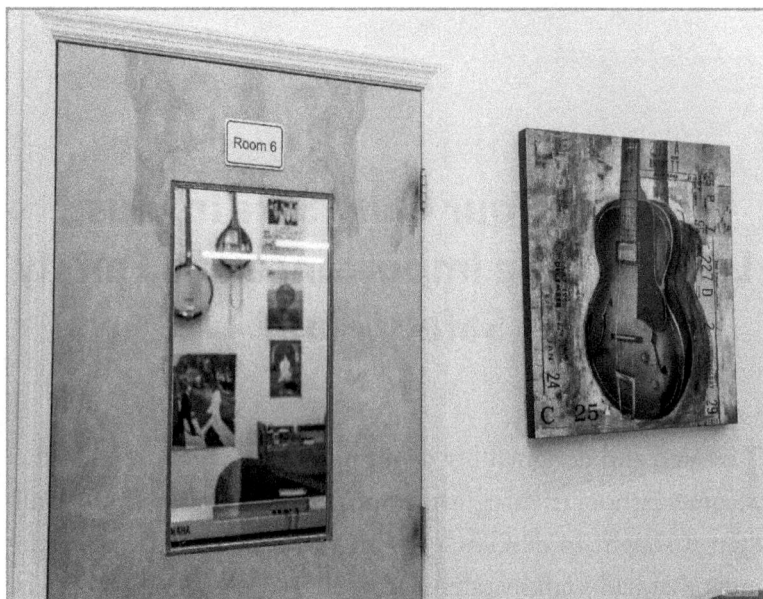

2. **Office Staff:** At my music academy, we require office staff to be present during lessons. Many other music academies have tight budgets and cannot afford the extra expense of employing office staff. This means that a student and a teacher might be unsupervised together in a lesson at 7:00 at night. In my opinion, this is not a safe practice and is irresponsible on the part of the academy. My academy always has office staff present so that students are never left alone with teachers.

3. **Background Checks:** I require that teachers and staff members undergo extensive background checks. Our teachers are required to pass four tests: a National Sex Offender Search, Statewide Criminal Background Check, National Criminal Background Check, and Social Security Number Verification. We view this as a necessary measure to preserve the safety and integrity of our academy.

4. **Security Cameras:** The safety of our students is our top priority, so we have security cameras in every single room. The precautionary program may be costly to the academy, but such a feature is worth it if it keeps our students safe and gives the parents peace of mind.

5. **Open-Door Policy:** Our school has an open-door policy for parents, which means that they're invited to sit in on their child's lessons. This should be something you look for when selecting an appropriate music school for your family.

6. **Open Floor Plan:** Our school has an open floor plan to provide an uncluttered and pleasant experience for our students and parents. We have ample seating in the hallways for families so that they can sit and watch their child's lesson through our glass windows (if they do not want to sit in on a lesson). I advise you to avoid schools that have hard-to-access classrooms. It is best to choose an academy that has an open space for everybody to see each other.

Whether you're looking to enroll your student in my music school or plan to find another, I recommend that you ensure the academy enforces each of the above safety plan features. My academy values these safety measures because we consider the children and students the top priority.

Chapter 11.

The Importance of Recitals

Giving an adult or child music student the opportunity to perform on stage every six months is extremely beneficial to the learning process.

First, it's the best way to get an honest assessment of how a student is progressing. Many parents need to see the improvements their child is making from week-to-week. Unfortunately for eager parents, progress isn't always consistent. If you were to reference any stock graph, you'd see that companies have performance peaks and valleys performance.

In much the same way, there are peaks and valleys in a student's musical performance over time. Students will experience valleys during their practice sessions at home and peaks during their lessons at school. For this reason, recitals are important because you'll be able to see how your child is able to perform a particular piece they have dedicated their time to learning and perfecting.

The second benefit of recitals is that it gives students the chance to perform in front of an audience. These performances can play a big role in their self-confidence later in life when they will need to make in-class presentations, perform speeches, lead a meeting, run a church gathering, or give a full-blown sales presentation or conference. A recital helps them understand the importance of preparing and practicing for a performance in front of a real audience.

Another benefit of a recital is that the unexpected can happen. Mistakes, unforeseen sound issues, or missed cues have happened to every professional musician. For example, Metallica and Lady Gaga played at the Grammys and the microphone went out. Monumental sound issues have affected Super Bowl performances in front of millions of viewers. These professional artists were forced handle the situations tactfully and gracefully. Experiencing an unexpected mishap on stage will help the student learn how to react to problems, cope with stress, and improvise!

Recitals are great for boosting a child's self-esteem. Students are encouraged to invite their family, friends, and neighbors to their performances. A child has a lot to gain from having a room full of people they love watch them perform. For many, the pride and feeling of accomplishment of playing in front of a supportive crowd cannot be beaten.

It's important that a music academy places a heavy emphasis on having fun on the night of a recital. When you're researching music schools in your area, look for one that provides additional services that make the performance night a unique experience for your child.

At my school, we roll out a red carpet and have a step and repeat banner for our students, allowing them to take pictures with their families and teachers. Photos on a red carpet with a child's teacher are a memorable and confidence-boosting experience.

Our recitals are formal, and we encourage the students to dress up for the evening. The entire audience of families and friends acts as a supportive and positive network that uplifts and encourages the children on stage. Formal recitals are more beneficial than little showcases for children because they are given the opportunity to perform on a big stage with other performers in front of a large, enthusiastic crowd. While it is a good idea to choose a great academy with a positive and uplifting philosophy towards recitals, it's equally as important that you as a parent have an optimistic view of the recital. I am a very patient person, and I enjoy spending time with my three-year-old daughter and helping other children develop their own musical abilities. I understand that children are their own people and develop at their own rate, both in maturity and skill level.

It is with this mentality that I invite parents to be forgiving with their children during their recitals. Despite months of preparation and practice, many students are still quite nervous before a recital. If they truly aren't ready and aren't willing to go on stage, give them a hug, be supportive, and let them watch the other students perform.

Not being able to perform at a recital isn't the end of the world. Parents should be happy that they're investing in their children and giving them the opportunity to take lessons, perform, and grow. If a child doesn't wish to perform, then it isn't wise to force them to get on stage. They will always have another opportunity (often in six more months!) to prepare and perform on stage.

While I understand that parents want their children to be successful, I ask that parents allow their child's passion for music to grow in a healthy and organic way. Parents shouldn't push their child too hard because it could negatively impact their self-esteem. If your child makes a mistake on stage, it's important to be supportive of them and remind them that they'll have another opportunity soon.

My school is not a competitive environment, and we make sure that the students understand the importance of respecting and supporting each other. It's about the love of art and the musical journey.

In my years as a music professional and educator, I have seen children grow from shy and introverted to outgoing, confident young adults. The ones who underwent this change stuck with the lessons and took every recital opportunity they could. The students were inspired by music and they were able to perform in front of a crowd, which in turn boosted their confidence. The progress didn't happen after just four lessons, but from years of positive reinforcement by teachers and parents.

Chapter 12.

The Importance of Achievement Programs

Achievement programs give a child the opportunity to dream of improving their abilities, work toward a goal, and feel accomplished when they have mastered new skills. My school offers achievement programs for children to work toward. These programs provide incentives for children to practice consistently and take the learning process seriously.

Many schools offer music lessons that are private and exclusive. This approach is problematic because it is beneficial for students to participate in group classes and be around other students who are at different levels in their musical development. I advise parents to let their child participate in group singing, group guitar, and group piano lessons at their school. Although the bulk of their lessons will be one-on-one sessions with a teacher, a group lesson will provide your child with a point of reference on how they are doing.

To encourage students to continue to grow beyond their lessons, I created the Musical Ladder System® which is now used by 30,000 music students in the U.S., Canada, and Australia.

In this system, a student will complete a test for their teacher every three months. The curriculum is not standardized and the teacher has the ability to test the student on whatever they choose. Even though several students may have the same teacher, they will each receive a different test customized to their skill level and ability. If a child passes the test, they receive a wristband, and at certain levels, the children are awarded trophies and certificates of achievement.

These achievement programs are beneficial because give students a tangible token that reflects their success. The wristbands, trophies, and certificates can be displayed in the home and they often serve as an encouraging reminder of their hard work. We also have a parent portal online that parents log into and monitor their children's progress. We make a conscious effort to keep the communication between the teacher, parent, and student open, with an emphasis on encouragement.

When researching schools, be sure to select one with an achievement program of some sort. My school does not charge for these services, and there are no achievement fees. The recitals, trophies, wristbands, and certificates are all included in our enrollment cost.

Unfortunately, many schools charge for these programs, and it can be quite expensive if you have multiple children. Also, be wary of schools with unusually cheap tuition, as they will often tack on additional fees for trophies, awards, or participation in recitals to make up for it.

Chapter 13.

More About Guitar Lessons

The primary indication that a child is ready for guitar lessons is if they can sit through a 30-minute lesson. We can start guitar lessons at age five if the teacher feels the student is ready. It is usually best to use the school's instrument for a student's first lesson. The first lesson is a "test run", and the child and parent can decide if they want to continue with guitar and purchase their own instrument for the next lesson. I do not recommend buying an instrument before starting lessons, no matter how insistent or determined a child may be.

When you're looking to buy a guitar, I recommend buying a half-sized guitar for children. Your child's teacher will be able to recommend the appropriate instrument size depending on your child's size and height. A guitar with nylon strings (as opposed to steel strings) is also a great option. Nylon strings are much easier for a child to hold down because they're gentler on the fingers. You must also be aware of a guitar's action. Action is the height from the string to the fretboard. The higher the action, the harder it is to press down. A guitar with lower action is easier to press and will be more comfortable for your child to play on.

A sales associate at a music retailer can help guide you in the direction of a half-sized guitar with low action and nylon strings. I do not recommend purchasing a cheap instrument, because a poorly-crafted instrument may lead to injuries. Commonly-reported injuries can include carpal tunnel or tendonitis. Save your time and money, and reduce your potential for frustration by going to an expert and seeking their advice on a suitable guitar for your child.

If your child asks for a guitar as a present but hasn't taken a lesson yet, I recommend waiting before making the purchase.

Rather than giving the child a guitar, you can set up an appointment at a music school, give your child a card with a print out of a picture of a guitar, and tell them that you've arranged for a lesson.

During the first lesson, their teacher will recommend what guitar to get. This way, your child's anticipation will build, and they will have an incentive to try something new and challenging.

Prospective students and parents often ask if they should start on an electric or acoustic guitar. I would say that for an older child (aged 8 or above) or a teenager, an electric guitar is appropriate. If the electric guitar has the right action, it might be easier to start on because they're more responsive to the touch.

In the end, selecting the right type of instrument depends on the student's interest. If your child loves rock music and that is the genre they are interested in, there's nothing wrong with starting on an electric guitar.

Playing an instrument should be fun and exciting. **It should never hurt your child's fingers to play a guitar**. If your child is complaining that an instrument is painful or excessively fatiguing to play, then you should get them a different guitar.

One reason people experience pain in their fingers while playing guitar is that they're pressing down on the strings too hard or they're attempting chords that are not appropriate for their skill-level.

As a beginner, it is important to not over-practice. Just as you would not begin golf lessons and risk injuring your shoulder by practicing two hours a day, a child does not need to practice guitar for hours on end. I recommend that working up from 10–20 minutes a day is acceptable for a beginner.

Chapter 14.

Details About Piano Lessons

Our piano instructors teach a variety of styles, from classical to pop music. Whether your child wants to learn Bach or Alicia Keys, our teachers are happy to help them become the pianist they dream of being. Our piano instructors will teach your child the fundamentals of sight reading, technique, and theory, but they will also incorporate their favorite songs into the lessons. You don't have to have a piano at home for your child to take lessons. A simple full-size electronic keyboard will suffice for the first six months. Our piano teachers have warm personalities and enjoy sharing their love for the piano with all students.

Parents should have the instrument that the child is learning in music school available in the home. Having the instrument in the space where a child spends much of their time will act as a reminder to practice. If a child is just beginning to learn piano, department stores have medium- or full-sized keyboards that are quite affordable. I recommend having a keyboard at home for at least six months or until after their first recital. If things are going well and the child is enjoying their lessons, you can look into getting a piano or a nicer keyboard.

There is also the option of renting a piano from a music store. Many people also will give away their unused piano for free as long as you handle the pick-up and transportation. You will need to hire a mover to transport the piano and a professional tuner to tune it once it has been placed in your home. One of the advantages of renting a piano is that the retail store will be able to move the piano for you. If you plan to obtain a piano, communicate with your child and ensure that they're committed to playing in the future. Pianos need to be periodically tuned and shouldn't be neglected. Pianos should be tuned once a year for optimal sound.

If you have questions or need advice on purchasing an instrument, music retailers and musical schools are great resources. Music store staff and the teachers at my music academy are very informed on the implications of purchasing or renting a music instrument, whether it be a guitar or a piano, and they will guide you through the process.

If you are looking to take on a used, 50-year-old acoustic piano, I advocate that you seek the advice of a specialist. If they tell you that the piano is not in good condition and won't function well, then I wouldn't buy it. The cost of tuning and getting it working properly may cost more than a newer or well-maintained piano.

Source: pixabay.com

MORE THAN MUSIC

Chapter 15.

Details About Voice Lessons

Many teachers and schools have different philosophies about the right age for a child to begin voice lessons. Our students can start taking voice lessons at age six. My best advice for the parents of children starting voice lessons is to be patient with your child because the voice takes time to develop.

When starting voice lessons, a teacher will start the student off with songs that are in the appropriate range. Many students are frustrated by voice lessons because they are impatient. Just like exercising in a gym, if you want to get stronger, you must realize that it will take practice and time to achieve this goal. The principle is the same with voice lessons; your child is going to the musical gym to slowly develop their skills.

Voice lessons require work on the student's range and ear. Many voice students are insistent on seeing quick and immediate results, but I often remind them that making progress with the voice usually takes longer than those who are learning other instruments. If a student wants to become a great singer, they will have to stay committed to the practice. Many vocalists also focus on physical fitness and health in order to maintain a clear and strong voice. I recommend that voice students be mindful of the commitment and willpower that is required of the pursuit.

Voice lessons require few expenses; you may need books or music materials, but the majority of the process entails the student being patient in their practice. Record your child's voice on the computer and play it back several times. Have the child listen to their voice and track their progress over time to see how they have improved.

Your child can also expect to have a variety of exercises and activities to improve their vocal abilities. The student will practice breathing and stretching exercises and activities to work on their range, tone, the shape of their mouth, and tongue placement. It is wise to find a teacher who is willing to work on music your child is interested in. Voice students must have realistic goals with themselves and their teachers.

𝄞 MORE THAN MUSIC

Chapter 16.

Details About Drum Lessons

At my music school, you don't need to buy a drum set as a beginner drum student. Instead, students purchase drum sticks, books, and a drum practice pad, which is an inexpensive percussion tool that allows students to practice their exercises and songs. Many parents mistakenly believe that that their child's drum playing will be loud and unpleasant in the home. On the contrary, percussion pads are much quieter than a full drum set.

Once your child has made it through a recital and has been practicing for at least six months, they may be ready to work up to another drum option.

The first option is electric drums that allow the student to play and hear the sounds through headphones and not disturb others or harm their own hearing.

The second option for those students who are displaying exceptional talent is to move to an acoustic drum set. I only recommend this option once the student has discussed it with their teacher, excelled with the practice pads, and successfully utilized the electronic kit for some time.

For those concerned about the noisiness of drums, there are various tools to deaden the sound of acoustic drum playing, such as mesh heads, cymbal silencers, and thistle sticks.

Chapter 17.

The Difference Between Method Books and Repertoire Books

There are two main types of music books that your child will be exposed to during their lessons.

The first are method books, which provide a student with the technique that should be used for playing their instrument. An analogy for a method book in music would be a book on golf that shows you how to swing the club and how to position your arms.

The second are repertoire books. These are songbooks like a Beatles songbook, a Disney songbook, or musical theater songbook.

Parents should encourage their child's teacher to use both types of books during their lessons. I also advise parents to get as many books as they can because they allow the child to dive in and learn about what they need to know as students while they're outside of their lesson.

You should be wary of schools and teachers that do not assign new books to their students. As a parent, you should expect to not only sign up for lessons, but to also purchase the method and repertoire books the teacher recommends.

In the long term, a child isn't going to play scales during their recital; they're going to play something from their repertoire book, like "Hey Jude." However, if the student can't play scales, they can't play "Hey Jude." For this reason, both types of books are essential for all levels of music students.

MORE THAN MUSIC

Chapter 18.

What to Expect During the First Lesson and on the Ride Home

(And Why Not to Get Angry at Your Teacher About It)

During the first lesson, a teacher will place more emphasis on getting to know your child than teaching them to play their new instrument. The best use of a teacher's time is learning about the child's interest in music, their personality, work ethic, and what they hope to get out of music lessons.

Once the teacher, parent, and child have talked for the majority of the lesson, the teacher may open a book and begin on page one with the student. It is important that parents feel comfortable asking questions and devising a personalized plan for their child during the first lesson.

There is often a stark difference between what a parent wants to hear on the ride home and what they actually get from their child. A parent usually wants a long, detailed discussion about everything that happened, described from A-Z and communicated on a relatively high adult level. It's natural for parents to want this type of response because they're curious about how the lesson transpired and how the child felt about it.

However, parents need to understand where their child is at developmentally. Many children are quiet by nature, and they will not engage in a long conversation on any topic. Others may be more talkative about things they're interested in, be it games, foods, or friends. Most children, however, are likely not interested in a discussion about different major and minor scales, chords, and the fundamentals of music.

Parents will often get in the car with their child and ask, "How did the lesson go?" To which the child responds, "Fine." From there, the parent may become frustrated because they expect details. You may wonder if something went wrong in the lesson and begin to worry. You must remember that at their maturity level, children cannot communicate the same way that adults do. It doesn't mean that anything went wrong with the lesson or that they're unhappy with the school.

Children can't participate in an adult-like conversation about their lesson because they are not adults. Parents can instead find fulfillment by being involved in the process in other ways. If you attend the last few minutes of each lesson and have a good, open relationship with the teacher, you won't need to worry about your child's lack of discussion immediately after a lesson.

Chapter 19.

How to Measure Progress

Student success is highlighted during recitals and through achievement programs, such as my Musical Ladder System®.

Be sure to communicate regularly with your teacher and listen in on the last five minutes of your child's lesson. My school has parent portal software, and I encourage parents to utilize this resource. Log in, read the teacher's practice notes, and consider them as an indication of your child's progress.

One of the best things a child can do is to practice their instrument at home. If they are young or new to the instrument, their practice sessions may last from five to ten minutes at first. As time goes on and the child improves, they may eventually practice for 20 or 30 minutes. Consider this: If your hobby is golf, and you get busy for two weeks and can't play, are you going to throw your golf club in the lake and forget about it? Or are you going to resume when your schedule permits? Children deserve the same respect and level of patience that you would give yourself.

There are currently 115 schools in the U.S. and Canada that utilize the Musical Ladder System® with their students. Choose a school that uses the System (you can see a full list of schools in your area at musicalladder.com) and allows for children to see breakthroughs in their progress every three months. It's important for kids to be rewarded at certain levels so that they're continually engaged and motivated to perform better each week. To make sure that your child is progressing in their skills, follow my three-step action plan:

1. Ensure your child **takes achievement tests** every three months.

2. Allow your child to **participate in recitals** every six months.

3. **Pop into the last five minutes of the lesson** as often as you can.

This is a helpful action plan for any parent to follow during their child's musical journey. As a parent, you will be supportive enough if you follow these three steps. This requires faith in your teacher's curriculum and trust in the school's administration. If you follow these steps and discover that you aren't happy with the results, then find a different professional to work with your child.

At the end of the day, parents need to trust the process and feel good about it. Take it from someone who has been in the industry a long time, the process is incredibly strong and can allow for the parent and child to be happy. Parents from all backgrounds—whether it's a small business, corporate America, or military—can value being held accountable for one's work. We incorporate this philosophy into our curriculum.

Chapter 20.

The "One-Teacher Trap"

Throughout my years in the field, I have found that parents of music students occasionally fall into what I call the "one-teacher trap."

A music student will often have a single music teacher when they first start their musical journey. Over time, illness and family demands may force the teacher to miss lessons here and there. It is also not uncommon for teachers to relocate at some later date, forcing you to find a new teacher.

When a parent realizes that their child's regular teacher is temporarily or permanently unavailable, they may feel panic when their child is reassigned to a different teacher.

While it is certainly normal for a student and their family to grow close to a teacher over time, I often tell parents that a new teacher can provide a fresh perspective on their child's learning. The wonderful thing about changing music teachers over time is that students are given a new perspective, new advice, and recommendations for their performance. They also learn to communicate with different people of authority and they are better able to adapt to new teaching styles.

When the time comes to change music teachers, regardless of what the circumstance may be, I encourage you to view the situation as a potentially positive experience for your child. Think back to a moment in your past when a stable figure in your life that you were close and friendly with parted ways.

Perhaps you had a hair stylist or barber you quite liked who left the salon, or maybe you regularly enjoyed the sermons of a particular pastor who moved to another city, or perhaps you had a favorite sports coach who left your team.

It is natural to become attached to people we are familiar with and have spent time with. Now, I urge you to think of the individual who replaced the person you were once attached to. Many times we become even closer and more connected with the replacement. New people in our lives provide a boost of motivation that can be conducive to our personal growth and development. Another pastor could have a different style that challenges and intrigues you. A new sports coach can view your skill with fresh eyes and make helpful recommendations on your form, speed, or training methods. When it comes to music, a new teacher will have a new perspective that could be a better match for your child's skill set and practice methods. The new instructor could foster a new enthusiasm for their instrument.

I once had an adult student attend one of my music schools who regularly visited the same teacher. His teacher was not available one evening for their lesson so my staff arranged for the student to have a substitute teacher. When the student arrived and was notified in the lobby that he would have a substitute for the day, he became upset, began yelling, and stormed out of the school. He went home and wrote a lengthy email about how upset he was that his teacher was unavailable, and he eventually left the school.

However, if that student had actually attended his lesson, he would have been pleasantly surprised. We had arranged for the student's substitute to be the teacher who had mentored and taught his teacher many years ago. The substitute had more degrees than the student's regular teacher, had been teaching longer, and had more experience in the world of music. In the end, the student may have enjoyed his lesson and gained some valuable information. Had he been open to the idea of change, something positive probably would have come of it.

I believe students should have at least three or four teachers throughout their lives. Having the opinions of different people with different backgrounds will expose your child to a wider variety of information than if they were confined to the suggestions of a single teacher.

Chapter 21.

Signs Your Child Is Not Ready for Lessons

(And Why That's Okay)

The first signs that your child is not ready for music lessons will most likely come from their teacher or the administration at their music school. The teacher will send a message, make a call, or speak to you in person and inform you that your child has not been sitting down, listening, or being attentive during their 30-minute lesson.

Some parents become defensive or may be upset that their child does not have the patience for lessons yet. However, it is normal for a child's interest to stall or wane. Children can easily become distracted and lose interest in any task, and it is worth observing what they want or what their teacher is telling you.

On the other hand, a child's lack of desire to practice their instrument at home shouldn't immediately be seen as an indication of lost interest. During my own development, I didn't practice consistently or for extended periods of time after school, and I've enjoyed a great music teaching and performance career.

As a young music student, I took a break from playing. After I distanced myself from the violin and explored other interests, I came back to music with a fervent passion. Even though I temporarily stopped playing, this did not mean that I stopped enjoying music altogether. In fact, I have based my career around the music world and have made it my mission to share the rewarding and fulfilling benefits of music with children and adults.

A respectable school will express concern for your child and recommend you take a break rather than consider the amount of money they would lose by doing so.

A music school doesn't want to lose business by telling a parent their child is no longer interested, and it will be a difficult call for them to make. Parents should be appreciative of a school for their honesty when they make the ethically right decision to tell them the truth. If a teacher says a child will not sit still or is clearly not interested in lessons, then it is a waste of the family's money and time to continue paying for lessons. Feedback from the teacher is a most important tool when considering whether or not to take a break from music lessons.

Chapter 22.

The Parent FREAK-OUT: If They're Not Practicing, I'm Not Paying!

The "parent freak-out" usually occurs after a child has been in lessons for a couple of months. Parents are going about their busy lives when suddenly it hits them: "Hey, I have been paying for music lessons for quite some time now. Come in here and play something for me."

This is the equivalent of pulling a child onto a baseball field and saying, "I'm going to throw this ball at you, and I want you to hit a home run." This is not how progress is exhibited when children are learning a new skill, whether it is music, sports, or reading. Instead, you should be willing to listen when a child offers to play or wants to show you something new they have learned.

I have played guitar for 35 years and have taught for 25 years. One of my biggest pet-peeves as an adult is when people put me on the spot and ask me to play something for them. If someone is a writer by profession, you wouldn't put them on the spot and ask them to write something for you or ask a doctor you've just met to look at your injury or trouble an attorney friend to look at a contract of yours on a whim.

The parent freak-out comes from an honest place; parents want their investment to be put to good use. They're paying for their child's lessons, and they want to see that the tuition money they're paying is worth it. **It is important to remember that impromptu living room performances are not always a clear indication of a child's progress.**

Learning is an organic process, and the expression of learning should also be organic. By this I mean to say that a child should not be forced to play for anyone. Instead, be willing to listen when a child is proud of what they learned and want to show you.

You can also consider the upcoming recital as a perfect platform to see how your child is doing. I advise parents to wait for the recital to determine the development of their child's skills. If the recital occurs, and you're not happy with the results, then it's time to visit the school, approach the teacher, and voice your concerns.

I often hear parents say, "If they're not practicing, I'm not paying." If you look back at my childhood, you would see that I didn't practice much at all and just attended my lessons every week. From a math perspective, there are 48 lessons a year that each last 30 minutes. That is a total of 24 hours of lessons for music students. What is better for the child's mind and development: 24 hours of lessons in a year or zero? The obvious answer is 24 hours.

To go further into my example, I took piano and violin as a child, but hated group guitar. I didn't practice an hour a day as my teachers instructed and would purposefully pop my guitar strings when my teacher wasn't looking so I could go play outside. As an adult however, things changed. I now play for my town's New Year's Eve festival, which has an attendance of 30,000 people. I have played around the U.S. and in Europe. I went on to pursue a Master's degree in music and was a music professor for six years at the University of South Carolina Upstate and Midlands Technical College. If my parents hadn't encouraged music in the home and allowed me to progress at my own pace, I wouldn't be where I am today.

One of the most profound observations I have made is that whether the student is a child or an adult, just because they aren't practicing today doesn't mean they won't begin to practice in three months, six months, or a year from now.

The spark of motivation can by lit by a friend, movie, concert, song, or video at any moment in time. I often consider what my life would have been like had my mother stopped encouraging my interest music when I lost interest in the violin. I would have never been able to play guitar, and I probably wouldn't be where I am today.

The same principal applies to artists in the music industry. In the past, musicians would release a couple of albums before they broke through as part of their musical development. It wasn't until later in pop music history that corporations started to change this pattern and require that musicians have a hit early on in their career. What has happened to the music industry as a result? In all honesty, it is struggling as a direct result because they are not developing their artists. Parents would do well to be patient and allow their children to musically develop like the great musical artists have before them.

I advise parents to seriously consider the concept of patient, steady development as it applies to improvement in music. Resist the temptation to ask your child to conduct a full-blown concert for you. To avoid the parent freak-out, observe the beginning of a music lesson with the mindset that your child will commit a minimum of six months to their instrument. Within six months, you should be able to see signs of improvement, and this will help alleviate your urge to panic.

Choosing a school with an open-door policy that allows for parents to be in the loop is essential. I also recommend that parents turn off their phones, get out of their cars, and come inside and talk to their child's teacher before, during, or after a lesson.

If your child's lesson is from 4:30 pm to 5:00 pm, plan to come in five minutes before the lesson ends to listen to the child play, talk to the teacher, and use it as a time to wrap things up. These five minutes will not take away from the lesson, instead, they will be the best way to really know how your child is progressing.

Chapter 23.

Homeschooling and Music Lessons

Before researching music schools, I would advise parents who homeschool their children to check on the accreditation in their state to see if there is an arts requirement for their children. Identifying what you are required to do and what types of credit music lessons may qualify for academically is important for homeschool parents. If there are any tax advantages with satisfying a music credit, you should document the necessary information.

From there, you should find a school with a family safety plan in place; one that offers recitals and has a rewards system. These features can be especially useful for a homeschooled student because these children generally have more flexibility and availability than students enrolled in traditional schools.

Most music schools will conduct lessons during the middle of the day. This timeframe sees far fewer students than lessons during the late afternoons and evenings. With fewer people at the school, you and your family get the school to yourself, you have more time to get to know the office, and you are able to meet other parents.

You may find that you are able to better connect with the homeschool community in your area. Your child will also be able to achieve a harmonious balance between their homeschooling and social interactions at the music school. Homeschooled kids also deserve to be on the big stage during their recital and receive praise for their hard work.

For fathers who are looking to be more involved with their child's homeschooling, they can use music lessons to their advantage. It is often the mother who conducts the homeschooling while the father is at work. The child's father could take his lunch hour from work on Tuesdays to go home, pick up his child, take them to lessons, grab a bite to eat with them, and then go back to work. In this way, the father is involved with the child's learning each week. This will foster a deeper and more connected relationship.

If your family operates on a more consistent schedule, then you may find that Sunday afternoons are a great time for your child's music lessons. When my music school began offering Sunday lessons five years ago, we saw that they quickly became the most popular, highly-attended days of the week. Many families found that they were able to go to church, have lunch, and then go to their music lessons on Sunday afternoons.

My music school is purposefully set up to function as an inviting and comfortable place for families to spend time together. We have a kids' area with toys and learning tools so that the children can play together. There are comfortable chairs throughout the office allow visitors to spend quality time with others in the music school community.

At one of our locations, we have an outside space for children to play with chalk and for parents to sit in one of our twelve rocking chairs on the porch and supervise. At both locations, we provide tables so that children can do their schoolwork or parents can catch up on their own work during their child's lesson. I encourage you to find a music school that has a warm and welcoming space.

MORE THAN MUSIC

Conclusion

By reading this book and putting considerable thought into your child's music journey, you have already taken the most important initial steps. Armed with the tools and insights you've learned from this book, you are well-informed and can select the right school for your child. Once you have chosen one with a safety plan you respect, taken a tour, researched the facility online, or gotten a referral from a friend, the rest is in the hands of the school and its teachers. An extraordinary music school will not have restrictive contracts or difficult hoops to jump through. As we say at my academies, the process "is very easy to get started, just pick out a day and time for your first lesson." Now it's time to rock and roll!

A beautiful and stress-relieving aspect of signing your child up for music lessons is that there is little financial risk. The worst that can happen is that your child no longer wishes to play. As long as the school has a month-to-month payment plan, all you have to do is give a 30-day notice.

Music lessons are a wonderful way to enrich your child's emotional, social, and academic development. Music lessons, exposure to recitals, and positive, constructive feedback from teachers will leave a child with a newfound sense of confidence.

As a parent, you will get to spend quality time with your child and learn more about music yourself. Being involved in the whole process and encouraging your child's learning will create a deeper parent-child bond. If you attend the lessons and recitals, they will never be able to look back and say, "My parents didn't do that for me." They will know you did your best to provide them with a hobby and skill that interested them and yielded long-term benefits.

Time is wasting and childhood is finite! We only have so many days on Earth to try new things, learn new skills, and practice commitment to a task we enjoy. There's nothing to fear in allowing your child to take music lessons. The journey is fun and exciting, and it will allow your child to grow in ways you may not currently know are possible.

Find a school that meets the suggested guidelines in this book and make an appointment for next week. Distractions will continue to inundate our lives; it's important to set those aside and let your child be a priority.

Beginning the process is incredibly simple. By reading this book you are already well-prepared. You are clearly a parent that cares about your child and their development. Now it's time to make some music!

About the Author

Marty Fort is a guitarist, music instructor, small business owner, university music professor, seminar speaker, and business coach.

Marty received a Bachelor of Music in classical guitar performance from the University of North Carolina School of the Arts and a Master of Music in classical guitar performance from the University of South Carolina.

He has completed two European performance tours and received a research grant to spend a summer in Siena, Italy giving chamber music concerts throughout Tuscany. In 1995, he traveled to London and studied privately with Michael Lewin (Head of Guitar Studies at the Royal Academy of Music). He has performed in master classes for guitar professors from Yale University, the Manhattan School of Music, The University of Southern California, and the Cleveland Institute of Music.

He currently operates the largest community music school in the state of South Carolina the *Columbia Arts Academy* and the *Lexington School of Music*. The schools serve students studying guitar, voice, bass, drums and piano. Marty oversees 80 music teachers and is responsible for hiring and overseeing the teaching staff.

From 2005–2011, Marty joined the music faculty at the University of South Carolina Upstate and taught Applied Guitar. During his first year at Upstate, he tripled guitar enrollment and created new courses in Group Guitar, Guitar Ensemble, Music Business, and Introduction to Audio Recording. In 2007, the

USC Upstate Guitar Ensemble was featured in concert on SC ETV.

Marty has moderated music industry panels with guests ranging from Matt Pinfield of MTV to major label rock bands like Weezer and Crossfade. He has also given presentations on marketing to crowds of over 1,000 people. His annual music academy owner seminars have been attended by hundreds of music school owners from different countries.

His business coaching methods have led small business owners to see increased gross profits of up to 100% in as little as 12 months with the Music Academy Success System.

For more information about music lessons, contact:

Columbia Arts Academy

3630 Rosewood Drive
Columbia, SC 29205
803-787-0931
ColumbiaArtsAcademy.com
info@ColumbiaArtsAcademy.com

Lexington School of Music

226 Barr Road
Lexington, SC 29072
803-996-0623
LexingtonSchoolofMusic.com
info@lexingtonSchoolofMusic.com